# EVERY DAY
# COUPETAILS

BRIAN HART HOFFMAN
& BROOKE BELL

83 press

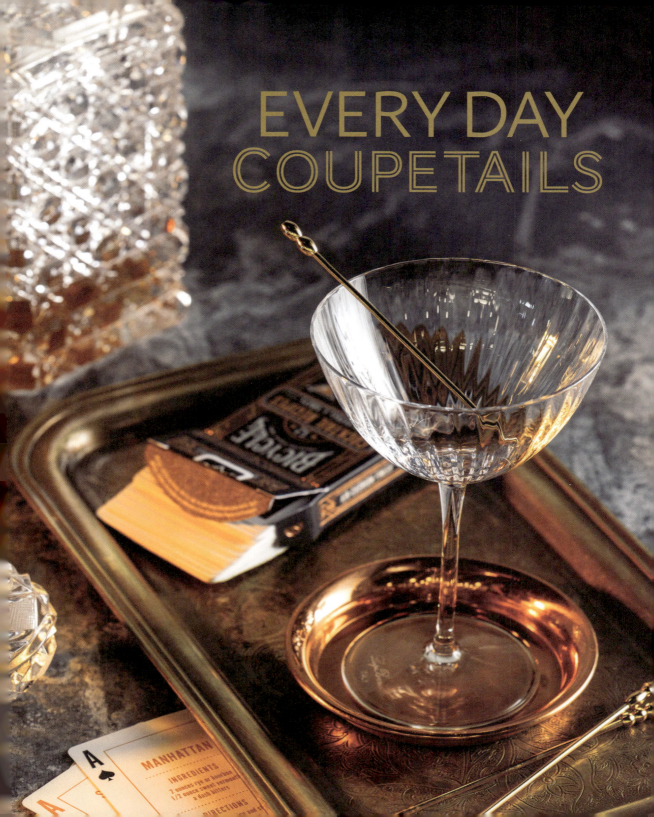

# EVERY DAY
# COUPETAILS

Copyright ©2025 by 83 Press

All rights reserved. No part of this book may be reproduced or transmitted in any form or by any means, electronic or mechanical, including photocopying, or by any information storage and retrieval system, without permission in writing from 83 Press. Reviewers may quote brief passages for specific inclusion in a magazine or newspaper.

83 Press
2323 2nd Avenue North
Birmingham, AL 35203
83Press.com

ISBN 979-8-9913469-4-8
Printed in China

## CONTENTS

- 8 INTRODUCTION
- 14 ALL DAYS
- 36 SUMMER DAYS
- 74 COOL AND CRISP DAYS
- 102 SWEET DAYS
- 132 ACKNOWLEDGEMENTS
- 134 INDEX AND NOTES

# INTRODUCTION

Before we even finished our last book, *Holiday Coupetails*, we were already dreaming up ideas for this one—because in our world, every day deserves a celebration. That's the beauty of cocktails: they can mark a moment, elevate an evening, or simply turn a regular day into something a little more magical.

As you flip through these pages, you'll start to see our cocktail personalities shine through. If there's gin, vodka, or rum in the mix, that's likely Brooke's influence. If it leans into bourbon, rye, or cherry, you're tasting Brian's favorites. And then there are the drinks that bring both of our tastes together—like the Concord Crush or Limoncello Spritz—that we're equally passionate about.

But above all, this book is a love letter to a very special piece of glassware: the coupe. Our affection for it just keeps growing, and nothing thrills us more than when a cocktail is served in one. There's also the thrill of the hunt, and we're always on the search for antique glasses that capture our hearts. There's something undeniably elegant—and glamourous—about the way a coupe cradles a drink. The coupe isn't just having a moment . . . it's having a movement. And trust us, it's here to stay.

Whether it's holding Champagne, a delicate cocktail, or even a dessert (we are bakers, after all!), the coupe glass is a must-have for your bar cart. Let's raise a coupe—because there's always something worth toasting.

Cheers! Santé! Cin cin! Salud! Prost! Skål!

—B + B
(Brian and Brooke)

# FAVORITE BAR TOOLS

Crafting a cocktail in a coupe glass isn't just about style—it's about precision and having the right tools at the ready. Bonus points if those tools are functional and beautiful! We might have a mild obsession with buying antique muddler spoons and cocktail shakers at our favorite brocantes in France. Whether you're shaking or stirring, the right gear makes all the difference.

**Cocktail shaker**
**Large mixing glass**
**Jigger**
**Muddlers and spoons**
**Bottle opener**
**Corkscrew**
**Cocktail strainer**
**Paring knife**
**Ice bucket**
**Cocktail skewers**
**Cocktail napkins**
**Citrus juicer**
**Vintage coupe glasses (a must!)**

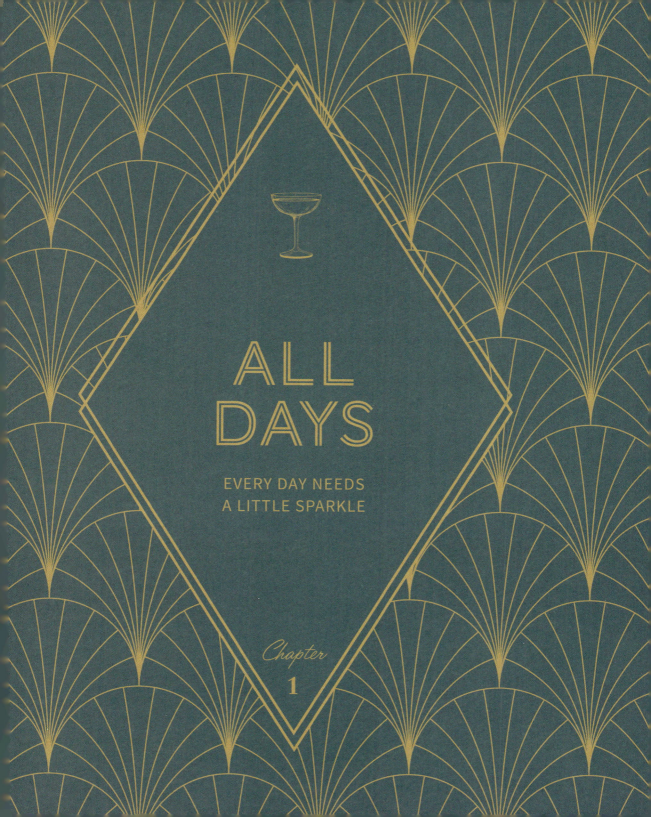

# THE WING VIEW

MAKES 1 SERVING

*We travel a lot hosting baking retreats around the world, and there's a cocktail tradition we never miss. On the flight home, we sip our signature in-flight cocktail that we've dubbed as The Wing View. All of the ingredients can be found on a beverage cart, and it's hard to mess it up. The color often matches our sunset view over the airplane's wing. —B+B*

2   ounces vodka
1   ounce cranberry juice, chilled*
½   ounce Simple Syrup (recipe on page 125)
**Club soda, chilled**

1. In a mixing glass, add vodka, cranberry juice, Simple Syrup, and ice. Stir until chilled. Strain into a coupe glass. Top with club soda.

*We used R.W. Knudsen Family Organic Just Cranberry Juice.

Note: Since airlines don't have the pure cranberry juice we prefer for a cocktail, this recipe includes simple syrup to mimic the juice cocktail they stock. If you want to use cranberry juice cocktail instead of pure cranberry juice, omit the simple syrup.

# DIRTY MARTINI

MAKES 1 SERVING

*I didn't drink my first martini until two years ago at the Ritz Paris' Hemingway Bar. Their olives frozen in ice cubes melt slowly and keep your cocktail icy cold. While it will forever be the best martini of my life, I've had some really good ones since then. Brian's husband, Stephen, makes a damn fine martini, and he's also a good partner in cocktail crime along with Emily Trotter. My order: Tito's or Grey Goose extra-dirty martini on the rocks. Bonus points for a sidecar of extra olive brine like what's served at The Milestone Hotel's Stables Bar in London.* —Brooke

2½ ounces vodka, chilled
1½ ounces olive brine*, to taste
½ ounce extra-dry vermouth
Garnish: Olive Ice Cubes (recipe on page 128)

1. Place coupe glass in freezer until chilled but not frosty, about 30 minutes.
2. In a cocktail shaker, add vodka, olive brine to taste, and crushed ice. Shake until cold.
3. Pour vermouth into chilled glass and swirl. Discard remaining vermouth. Strain vodka mixture into coupe glass. Garnish with Olive Ice Cubes, if desired.

*We used Filthy Olive Brine.

# THE ORANGE THING

MAKES 1 SERVING

---

*We're at that phase in life when we prefer a boozy lunch over a boozy dinner (hello . . . importance of a good night of sleep!), and there's no place we'd rather lunch than the patio of Bottega. You know you're living right when the sun is shining and The Orange Thing is delivered to your table.* —*B+B*

| | |
|---|---|
| 2 **ounces vodka** | 1. In a cocktail shaker, add all ingredients. Add ice and shake until cold. Strain into a coupe glass. |
| 2 **ounces fresh orange juice** | |
| 1½ **ounces triple sec** | |

Recipe courtesy of Pardis and Frank Stitt, Bottega, Birmingham, Alabama

# RABBIT RABBIT

## MAKES 1 SERVING

*The first day of each month brings "rabbit rabbit" wishes, an English tradition that's meant to bring good luck when you say it as soon as you open your eyes. My mother-in-law, Lorna, and I always compete to be the first to text each other. Sometimes, she sends a message in the middle of the night just so she can be first, and I see it as soon as I wake up. It's fitting that this cocktail features a favorite British tipple, Pimm's.* —Brooke

- 4 fresh strawberries, chopped
- 6 large fresh basil leaves
- 3 ounces Pimm's, chilled

Garnish: fresh strawberry, fresh basil sprig

1. In a cocktail shaker, muddle strawberries and basil. Add Pimm's and ice. Shake until cold. Strain into a coupe glass. Garnish with strawberry and basil, if desired.

# TOM COLLINS

MAKES 1 SERVING

*It's a classic for a reason. With only four ingredients, this easy-to-make cocktail is as refreshing as it is simple and won't ever go out of style. —B+B*

2 ounces dry gin
1 ounce fresh lemon juice
½ ounce Simple Syrup (recipe on page 125)
**Club soda, chilled**
**Garnish: lemon twist**

1. In a cocktail shaker, add gin, lemon juice, and Simple Syrup. Add ice and shake until cold. Strain into a coupe glass. Top with club soda. Garnish with lemon twist, if desired.

# FRENCH NEGRONI

MAKES 1 SERVING

*Bold, bitter, and effortlessly chic. This isn't just a coupetail—
it's a timeless statement. Santé! —B+B*

- 2 ounces Cognac
- 1¼ ounces Campari
- 1¼ ounces sweet vermouth
- 2 dashes El Guapo Spiced Cocoa Bitters
- 2 ounces Champagne, chilled

**1.** In a mixing glass, add Cognac, Campari, vermouth, bitters, and ice. Stir until chilled. Strain into a coupe glass. Top with Champagne.

# THE ENGLISH TEA

MAKES 1 SERVING

*Last fall, we finally got our Highclere Castle moment! Brian drove down country roads through wind and rain (on the left side, mind you!), and when we finally arrived at Highclere, we couldn't believe our eyes. We were staring at the Highclere Castle, the set of TV drama* Downton Abbey. *The place Brian's mom, Phyllis Hoffman DePiano, always dreamed of visiting. The theme music from the show played in our heads as we fought back tears walking toward the castle's storied front entrance. After a lovely meet and greet with The Countess of Carnarvon and private tour of the home, we learned that Highclere also makes gin with botanicals coming from the estate. This cocktail embodies two very British traditions: afternoon tea and high-quality gin. —B+B*

1½ ounces Highclere Castle gin
½ teaspoon loose-leaf jasmine tea
¾ ounce Luxardo Maraschino cherry syrup
½ ounce triple sec
1 dash orange bitters
**Garnish: lemon twist**

1. In a mixing glass, add gin and jasmine tea. Let sit for 30 minutes; strain through a fine-mesh sieve, discarding tea leaves.
2. In a cocktail shaker, add infused gin mixture, cherry syrup, triple sec, and bitters. Add ice and shake until cold. Strain into a coupe glass. Garnish with lemon twist, if desired.

*Recipe courtesy of Highclere Castle Gin*

# SABRINA

MAKES 1 SERVING

*A drink by any other name just wouldn't fit . . . Sabrina, a name that immediately takes me to my mother's side as we would sit and watch the movie (the Julia Ormond and Harrison Ford version is our fav!) for our mother-son date nights over and over again, never tiring of it. Now a cherished memory, I cling to and think of my mom each time I watch it. While Champagne is always a good idea, at least according to David Larrabee whilst famously meeting ladies for a dance in the solarium as the fabulous Larrabee parties continued on in the gardens, it was the love story that unfolded between Linus (David's brother) and Sabrina Fairchild, ultimately taking them to Paris, that inspired the cherry-hued ombré effect of this signature drink that solidifies "le temps des cerises" (cherry season) is year-round. With each sip, I can hear Sabrina's voice say, "I'm flying home," in reference to Paris, and that is a feeling I know all too well. —Brian*

- 1 ounce Cherry Reduction, chilled (recipe follows)
- 1 fresh cherry
- 6 ounces Champagne, chilled

1. In a coupe glass, add Cherry Reduction and cherry. Top with Champagne.

**CHERRY REDUCTION:** In a small saucepan, cook 1 cup tart cherry juice over medium-high heat until reduced by half, about 10 minutes, stirring occasionally. Remove from heat, and let cool completely. Place in an airtight container and chill until ready to use or up to 1 week.

# NITRO COLD BREW MARTINI

MAKES 1 SERVING

*OK, espresso martini fans . . . Replacing the traditional espresso with nitrogen-infused cold brew gives this pick-me-up a smooth texture that helps deepen the natural sweetness of the coffee flavor. P.S. We still can't drink a coffee martini after 4:00 p.m. —B+B*

2½ ounces vodka
1½ ounces coffee liqueur
2 ounces nitro cold brew
**Garnish:** coffee beans

**1.** In a cocktail shaker, add vodka, coffee liqueur, nitro cold brew, and ice. Shake until cold. Strain into a coupe glass. Garnish with coffee beans, if desired.

# END OF THE JAM JAR MARTINI

MAKES 1 SERVING

*Promise us one thing! You'll never throw away another jam jar with a smidge of flavor in the bottom. It's a cocktail just waiting to be shaken . . . in the jar. We love Bonne Maman for their quality and intense flavors. And if you've ever needed an excuse to purchase their epic Advent calendar, cocktail hour is your reason. Invite some friends over and let everyone shake up their coupe of choice! —B+B*

| | |
|---|---|
| 2 | ounces jam or preserves, flavor of choice (still in jar) |
| 2 | ounces vodka, chilled |
| ½ | ounce fresh lemon juice |
| ½ | ounce Simple Syrup (recipe on page 125) |

1. In jam jar with remaining preserves (see note), add vodka, lemon juice, and Simple Syrup. Add ice and shake until cold. Strain into a coupe glass.

*Note: If your jam jar isn't empty, add ingredients to cocktail shaker with 2 ounces of jam instead.*

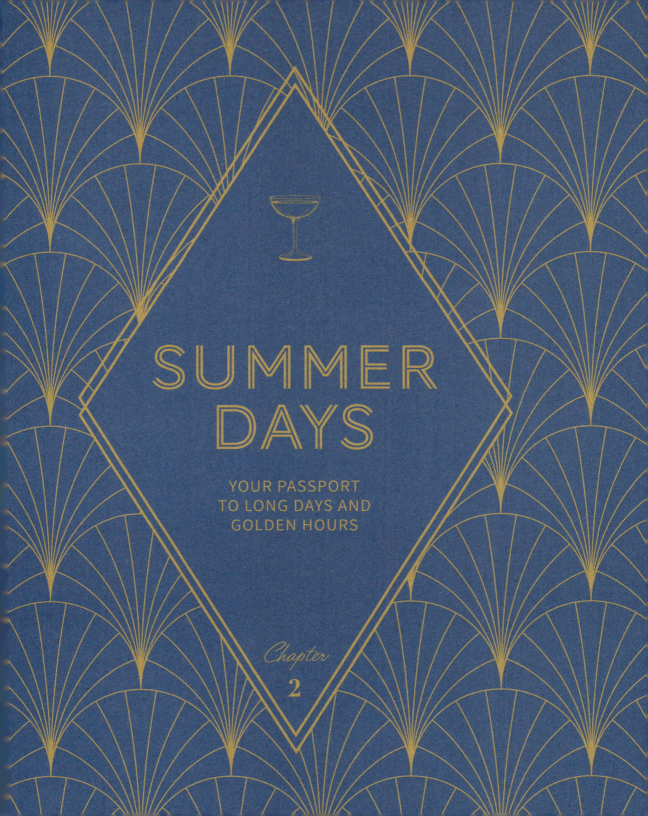
# SUMMER DAYS

YOUR PASSPORT TO LONG DAYS AND GOLDEN HOURS

*Chapter* 2

# BLUEBERRY LEMON DROP

MAKES 1 SERVING

*Blueberry Lemon Drops were my drink during the years that I called Seattle home . . . and not because the dark and rainy skies drove me to the brightness of this drink . . . it was the signature drink of West Five, a neighborhood restaurant that my best friend, Nathan, and I frequented for happy hour along with their epic mac and cheese . . . a perfect combo!* —Brian

1½ ounces vodka
½ ounce Blueberry-Vanilla Simple Syrup (recipe on page 126)
½ ounce triple sec
¾ ounce fresh lemon juice
**Garnish: fresh blueberries**

1. In a cocktail shaker, add vodka, Blueberry Simple Syrup, triple sec, and lemon juice. Add ice and shake until cold. Strain into a coupe glass. Garnish with blueberries, if desired.

# PEACH GIN SMASH

MAKES 1 SERVING

*Yes, I walk around The Market at Pepper Place in Birmingham, Alabama, eying Chilton County peaches for baking crostatas and crisps, but I'm also always thinking about cocktail hour, too. To be honest, there's not a fruit that I don't want to muddle in a cocktail shaker. This Peach Gin Smash is crisp, refreshing, and the perfect way to celebrate summer.* —Brooke

¼ ripe peach, peeled
½ teaspoon fresh lemon juice
1½ ounces gin
**Garnish: frozen peach slices**

**1.** In a cocktail shaker, muddle peach and lemon juice. Add gin and ice. Shake until cold. Strain into a coupe glass. Garnish with peach slices, if desired.

# TOMATO TINI

MAKES 1 SERVING

*We anxiously await tomato season each year, and now we've found the perfect way to drink our vegetables. Fresh tomato juice, vodka, basil leaves, and just a hint of salt make for a marvelous savory martini.* —B+B

| | |
|---|---|
| 2 | ounces vodka |
| 2 | ounces Tomato Liquid (recipe follows) |
| 2 | large fresh basil leaves |
| 1 | dash flaked sea salt |

Garnish: cherry tomatoes

1. In a cocktail shaker, add vodka, Tomato Liquid, basil, and salt. Add ice and shake until cold. Strain into a coupe glass. Garnish with tomatoes, if desired.

## TOMATO LIQUID

MAKES 1 CUP

| | |
|---|---|
| 1 | pound ripe red slicing tomatoes |
| ½ | teaspoon kosher salt |

1. In a blender, process tomatoes and salt until chunky. Using a fine-mesh sieve lined with cheesecloth, strain tomato mixture into a bowl overnight, discarding tomato solids. Store tomato mixture in an airtight container for up to 4 days.

# SPANISH GIN AND TONIC

MAKES 1 SERVING

*No exaggeration, the hottest I've ever been in my life was an August day after exploring Madrid in 100-degree heat. My husband, Andy, and I settled into our hotel bar with the air-conditioning blasting and had our first proper Spanish Gin and Tonic. My G&T game forever changed. The key, besides the region's lovely gins and small-batch tonics, is lemon! I'll never have a gin and tonic with lime again. —Brooke*

| | |
|---|---|
| 2 | ounces gin*, chilled |
| 4 | ounces club soda, chilled |
| ½ | ounce El Guapo Tonic Syrup, chilled |

Juniper berries, sichuan peppercorns, star anise, cardamom pods, whole cloves, sprigs fresh thyme, small fresh bay leaves, to taste

Garnish: lemon slices

1. In a mixing glass, stir together gin, club soda, tonic syrup, and spices to taste. Pour into a coupe glass. Garnish with lemon, if desired.

*We used Mahón Gin.

# BLACKBERRY BRAMBLE

MAKES 1 SERVING

*Many years ago, my friend Catherine came home from a summer in Italy and brought me a recipe for a cocktail she couldn't wait for me to try. I immediately started my blackberry vodka infusion, and after several weeks, Italy met Alabama blackberries. A year doesn't pass when I don't make a batch of Blackberry Vodka. I love watching the clear liquid turn to a brilliant purple.* —Brooke

2½  ounces Blackberry Vodka (recipe follows)
2  ounces club soda
Garnish: fresh blackberry, fresh rosemary sprig

1. In a mixing glass, add Blackberry Vodka and club soda. Add ice and stir until cold. Strain into a coupe glass. Garnish with blackberry and rosemary, if desired.

BLACKBERRY VODKA In a large glass jar or container with a lid, add 3 cups fresh blackberries and 4 cups vodka. (Vodka should completely cover blackberries.) Seal jar tightly. Place in a cool, dark place or in the refrigerator. Shake once a day for 2 weeks. Strain blackberry mixture, reserving blackberries or discarding. Boozy blackberries can be frozen and used to garnish future cocktails.

# PEACH DAYDREAM

MAKES 1 SERVING

*This low(er)-alcohol content cocktail will make you blush in the best way on warm summer days.* —B+B

| | |
|---|---|
| 4 | ounces Lillet Blanc |
| 4 | ounces peach nectar |
| 1 | ounce ginger liqueur |
| 2 | dashes El Guapo Barrel-Aged Vanilla Bitters |

**Garnish: fresh peach slice**

1. In a cocktail shaker, add Lillet Blanc, peach nectar, ginger liqueur, and vanilla bitters. Add ice and shake until cold. Strain into a coupe glass. Garnish with peach slice, if desired.

# BUSHWACKER

### MAKES 1 SERVING

*Recipes are memories. And memories are oftentimes recipes. I've wanted to recreate my dad's Bushwacker for years, and while he didn't leave me his recipe, he did leave a list of ingredients. This recipe has been reengineered by my taste memories of summer days on his wharf on Mobile Bay, where a Bushwacker was always a welcome treat. Thank you, Dad. I miss those days.* —Brooke

| | |
|---|---|
| 2 | ounces golden rum |
| 1 | ounce coffee liqueur |
| 1 | ounce dark crème de cacao liqueur |
| 1 | ounce cream of coconut |
| 2 | ounces half-and-half |
| 1 | cup ice cubes |

**1.** In a blender, add all ingredients and process until smooth. Pour into a coupe glass. Serve immediately.

# JARDIN SECRET

MAKES 1 SERVING

*Do you ever need a little prompt to remember that beautiful things grow in unexpected places? As a child, I can remember my grandfather "discovering" a blueberry bush that he'd planted years ago and had forgotten about. It was like a secret garden discovery with delicious benefits. What are you planting in your secret garden? As my friend Jane Bertch says of her jardin secret, "Growth takes time. It takes a long process to transform a seedling into a sprout and then into a beautiful flower," or in this case . . . a blueberry bush for cocktail hour.* —Brian

| | |
|---|---|
| 6 | fresh blueberries |
| 1 | ounce fresh lime juice |
| 2 | ounces vodka |
| 1 | ounce Blueberry-Vanilla Syrup (recipe on page 126) |
| 4 | ounces tonic water, chilled |

**Garnish: Blueberry Ice Cubes (recipe on page 128)**

1. In a cocktail shaker, muddle blueberries and lime juice. Add vodka, Blueberry-Vanilla Syrup, and ice. Shake until cold. Strain into a coupe glass. Top with tonic water. Garnish with Blueberry Ice Cubes, if desired.

# NOT FROZEN PIÑA COLADA

MAKES 1 SERVING

*There are days when you just want a piña colada for a mental escape, but you don't want the hassle of making a frozen drink. Enter the oh-so-clever Not Frozen Piña Colada. Close your eyes. Take a deep breath. Exhale relaxation.* —Brooke

| | |
|---|---|
| 4 | ounces Clarified Piña Colada (recipe follows) |
| 3 | dashes tiki bitters* |

1. In a cocktail shaker, add Clarified Piña Colada and bitters. Add ice and shake until cold. Strain into a coupe glass.

*We used El Guapo Polynesian Kiss Bitters.

**CLARIFIED PIÑA COLADA** In a large bowl, add 9½ ounces heavy whipping cream. In a separate medium bowl, combine 2 cups clear rum, 2 ounces Demerara Simple Syrup (recipe on page 126), 9½ ounces coconut water, 9½ ounces pineapple juice, and 5 ounces fresh lime juice. Slowly pour rum mixture into cream, stirring until curdled. Let stand at room temperature for 45 minutes. Drape a cheesecloth over a large bowl. Strain rum mixture through cheesecloth, squeezing excess moisture. (Liquid should be clear. If still cloudy, strain again through a clean cheesecloth.) Store in an airtight container in refrigerator for up to 1 week.

# LE VIE EN ROSÉ

MAKES 1 SERVING

*Paris is called the City of Light—and after experiencing one pink-hued sunset in this most fabulous city, you'll never see pink skies the same way again. Édith Piaf captured the magic of seeing life through rose-colored glasses in her song, "La Vie en Rose"—and now this cocktail will also take you there! Still rosé (preferably a dry Côte de Provençe) translates perfectly in this drink and nods to the calm feeling of lingering on the terrace of a Parisian bistro at sunset, under the rosy sky as the world passes you by. À la vôtre!* —Brian

| | |
|---|---|
| 1½ | ounces vodka |
| 1 | ounce Maraschino liqueur* |
| 2 | dashes vanilla bitters |
| ¼ | ounce Maraschino cherry syrup** |
| 1 | Maraschino cherry** |

Rosé wine, chilled***

1. In a mixing glass, add vodka, liqueur, bitters, cherry syrup, and ice. Stir until cold. Strain into a coupe glass and add cherry. Top with rosé wine.

*We used Luxardo Maraschino Originale.
**We used Luxardo Maraschino Cherries.
***We used Corbières Rosé Domaine de Fontsainte.

EVERY DAY COUPETAILS

# NOT SO SWEET TEQUILA SUNRISE

MAKES 1 SERVING

*The classic 1970s cocktail gets a 21st-century makeover with sweet cherries, Campari, and El Guapo Cuban bitters, resulting in a complex coupe you'll crave all summer long.* —B+B

| | |
|---|---|
| 2 | Maraschino cherries* |
| ½ | ounce cherry syrup* |
| 1 | ounce Campari |
| 3 | ounces fresh orange juice, chilled |
| 2 | ounces tequila |
| 2 | dashes El Guapo Cuban bitters |

1. In a small bowl, stir together cherries, syrup, and Campari; set aside.
2. In a mixing glass, add orange juice, tequila, and bitters. Add ice and stir until chilled. Strain into a coupe glass. Slowly top with cherry mixture, letting it sink to the bottom.

*We used Luxardo Maraschino Cherries and syrup.

# LIMONCELLO SPRITZ

MAKES 1 SERVING

*When you fall in love with the island of Capri, you fall hard. And sipping on a Limoncello Spritz in the late afternoon as the streets begin to quieten certainly helps you quickly fall in love with this unique island that's truly like no other. Our friends Holly Star and Gianluca D'Esposito, who host cooking classes at their villa, shared their limoncello recipe with us so we can "spritz" at home when we need to be in a Capri state of mind. —B+B*

2 ounces Limoncello (recipe follows), chilled
3 ounces Champagne, chilled
1 ounce club soda, chilled
**Garnish:** lemon slice

1. In a coupe glass, add Limoncello, Champagne, and club soda. Garnish with lemon slice, if desired.

LIMONCELLO Pour 4 cups of grain alcohol into an airtight container with the peel of 10 lemons. Cover with a tea towel and place in a dark place for a minimum of 3 weeks. Boil 5 cups water in a large pot. Add 4 cups granulated sugar, stirring until it dissolves. Let cool. When simple syrup is lukewarm, place a fine-mesh sieve over pot. Strain alcohol mixture into pot of simple syrup, discarding lemon peels. Stir, let cool. Strain into another large pot before funneling into bottles. Store in a dry, cool, dark space for 2 to 3 weeks before storing in the freezer.

*Limoncello recipe adapted from Michel'angelo Capri*

# STRAWBERRY SPARKLER

### MAKES 1 SERVING

*Bubbly and totally irresistible—strawberry, Aperol, and Champagne mix for a sip that's sweet with just the right amount of sass.* —B+B

2 ounces Strawberry Purée (recipe follows), chilled
2 ounces Aperol, chilled
6 ounces Champagne, chilled
Garnish: Strawberry Ice Cubes (recipe on page 128)

1. In a coupe glass, add Strawberry Purée and Aperol. Top with Champagne. Garnish with Strawberry Ice Cubes, if desired.

## STRAWBERRY PURÉE
### MAKES ¾ CUP

1 cup fresh strawberries, washed and hulled

1. In the work bowl of a food processor, add strawberries; process until smooth. Chill until ready to use. Store up to 1 week.

# PEACH OLD FASHIONED

MAKES 1 SERVING

*Don't get confused, bourbon isn't a seasonal drink relegated to the cold and dark days of autumn and winter. This bright and fresh take on an Old Fashioned might just make this the "new fashioned" drink of your summer! Bold peach flavor is made even brighter by the lemon juice and orange bitters . . . so be bold and bring bourbon into the brighter days with this coupetail. —Brian*

- 2 ounces rye bourbon
- 1 ounce Peach Simple Syrup (recipe on page 126)
- ½ ounce fresh lemon juice
- 2 dashes orange bitters

Garnish: fresh peach slices

1. In a mixing glass, add bourbon, Peach Simple Syrup, lemon juice, and bitters. Add ice and stir until cold. Strain into a coupe glass. Garnish with peach slices, if desired.

# RUM REVERIE

MAKES 1 SERVING

*The classic daiquiri, in its original form, is a simple three-ingredient cocktail that's tart, sweet, and a whole vibe in a glass. —B+B*

| | |
|---|---|
| 2 | ounces island rum* |
| ¾ | ounce fresh lime juice |
| ¾ | ounce Simple Syrup (recipe on page 125) |

Garnish: lime slice

1. In a cocktail shaker, add rum, lime juice, and Simple Syrup. Add ice and shake until cold. Strain into a coupe glass. Garnish with lime slice, if desired.

*We used Havana Club Puerto Rican Rum.

# SUNSET SIZZLE

MAKES 1 SERVING

*Smoky, sweet, and dangerously smooth — Mezcal and Homemade Grenadine unite for the ultimate surprise and delight! —B+B*

| | |
|---|---|
| 2½ | ounces Mezcal |
| 1 | ounce fresh lime juice |
| 1 | ounce Homemade Grenadine (recipe follows) |
| 4 | dashes Angostura bitters |

1. In a cocktail shaker, add Mezcal, lime juice, Homemade Grenadine, and bitters. Add ice and shake until cold. Strain into a coupe glass.

## HOMEMADE GRENADINE
MAKES 1 CUP

- ½ cup pomegranate juice
- ½ cup granulated sugar

1. In a medium saucepan, bring all ingredients to a boil over medium heat, stirring occasionally. Boil for 1 minute. Let cool completely. Refrigerate in an airtight container for up to 1 month.

# IN A PICKLE

MAKES 1 SERVING

*The first time we came across this brilliant cocktail idea on social media, we immediately shared photos with each other and knew a version had to be included in this book. For all the skeptics out there, it works! The kick from the peppercorns and pickle juice is downright daring, and once you start . . . you can't stop sipping.* —B+B

3 pink peppercorns
2 tablespoons fresh dill sprigs
2 ounces London dry gin
2 ounces pickle juice*
Club soda, chilled
Garnish: fresh dill sprigs, pickle slices, pink peppercorns

1. In a cocktail shaker, muddle peppercorns and dill. Add gin, pickle juice, and ice. Shake until cold. Strain into a coupe glass. Top with club soda. Garnish with dill, pickles, and peppercorns, if desired.

*We used Grillo's Pickles.

# ORANGE HIBISCUS MARGARITA

MAKES 1 SERVING

*This vibrant margarita reminds us of the colorful streets of San Miguel de Allende, Mexico, a city like no other, and a favorite place for sipping cocktails in the shadows of the majestic Parroquia de San Miguel Arcángel. —B+B*

4   ounces blanco tequila, divided
Hibiscus Sugar (recipe follows)
½   ounce orange liqueur
1   ounce fresh lime juice
1   ounce fresh orange juice
1   ounce hibiscus syrup*
Crushed ice

1. In a shallow bowl, pour 2 ounces tequila. In another shallow bowl, add Hibiscus Sugar. Dip the rim of the coupe glass in tequila and then in Hibiscus Sugar. Let dry.
2. In a cocktail shaker, add remaining 2 ounces tequila, orange liqueur, lime juice, orange juice, and hibiscus syrup. Add ice and shake until cold. Strain into prepared glass. Serve immediately.

*We used Shaker & Spoon Hibiscus Syrup.

## HIBISCUS SUGAR
MAKES ½ CUP

¼   cup pure hibiscus tea leaves
¼   cup granulated sugar

1. Place all ingredients in the bowl of a food processor, and process until well combined, about 1 minute. Store in an airtight container for up to 1 month.

# COOL AND CRISP DAYS

FOR WHEN THE AIR
TURNS BRISK AND
THE VIBES GET COZY

*Chapter*

3

# STEPHEN'S GINGER MARTINI

MAKES 1 SERVING

---

*My husband, Stephen, has become a martini drinking man over the last few years, and this creation is one of his best! Our neighbors, Susan and Andy, must have "shaker-level hearing," because once this drink is in the shaker, a social gathering isn't far behind.* —Brian

| | |
|---|---|
| 2½ ounces vodka or London dry gin | 1. In a cocktail shaker, add vodka or gin, ginger liqueur, Grand Marnier, and Lillet Blanc. Add ice and shake until cold. |
| 1½ ounces Domaine de Canton ginger liqueur | |
| 1 splash Grand Marnier | 2. Pour vermouth into a chilled coupe glass and swirl. Discard remaining vermouth. Strain vodka or gin mixture into prepared glass. |
| 1 splash Lillet Blanc | |
| ½ ounce white dry vermouth | |

# SPICED LILLET ROUGE

MAKES 1 SERVING

*You might be familiar with Lillet Blanc, but Lillet Rouge offers a deeper, richer flavor full of dark fruits and delicate spices. Topped with Champagne, this cocktail is a bubbly delight perfect for the first cool days of fall. —B+B*

2   ounces Lillet Rouge
1   ounce Cointreau or Grand Marnier
1   ounces Spiced Simple Syrup
    (recipe on page 126)
2   ounces Champagne, chilled
Garnish: star anise

1. In a mixing glass, add Lillet Rouge, Cointreau or Grand Marnier, Spiced Simple Syrup, and ice. Stir until cold. Strain into a coupe glass. Top with Champagne. Garnish with star anise, if desired.

# PEAR THYME GIMLET

**MAKES 1 SERVING**

*A master class in simplicity, the classic gimlet is revitalized with the herbaceous infusion of fresh thyme and the sweet, buttery flavor of pear.* —B+B

1 teaspoon fresh thyme leaves
2 ounces dry gin
1 ounce Pear Thyme Simple Syrup (recipe on page 127)
½ ounce fresh lemon juice
Garnish: whole pear slice

1. In a cocktail shaker, muddle thyme. Add gin, Pear Thyme Simple Syrup, lemon juice, and ice. Shake until cold. Strain into a coupe glass. Garnish with pear slice, if desired.

# CONCORD CRUSH

MAKES 1 SERVING

*This cocktail is based on one that's served at Gramercy Tavern in New York City. If our travels take us to the city in the fall, a barstool visit for their Concord grape cocktail is a must, not to mention taking in their incredible seasonal décor. When we're at home, we both scour our local grocery stores for Concord grapes and text each other when they are found. The season is short, so grab them the minute you see them in the stores or at your farmers' market if you're lucky enough to live where they are grown. —B+B*

- 2 ounces vodka
- 1½ ounces Concord Grape Purée (recipe follows)
- ½ ounce fresh lime juice
- ½ ounce Thyme Simple Syrup (recipe on page 127)
- 1 large pasteurized egg white

Garnish: fresh thyme leaves

1. In a cocktail shaker, add vodka, Concord Grape Purée, lime juice, Thyme Simple Syrup, and egg white. Add ice and shake until cold. Strain into a coupe glass. Garnish with thyme, if desired.

**CONCORD GRAPE PURÉE** In a blender, add 1 cup Concord grapes and 3 tablespoons fresh lime juice; pulse until grapes are split open and breaking apart, releasing juices. Strain through a fine-mesh sieve. Remove and discard seeds and skin. Place in an airtight container and refrigerate until chilled, about 20 minutes. Store in refrigerator for up to 1 week.

# ROSEMARY MEYER LEMON GIN FIZZ

MAKES 1 SERVING

*Each Christmas, my mom brings me loads of fresh Meyer lemons from Baldwin County, Alabama, where she lives on the Gulf Coast. We use them in as many recipes as we can during the holidays, but, inevitably, I'm always left with Meyer lemons to use into January. When I can't bake any more Meyer lemon loaf cakes, I juice the remaining lemons and freeze them into ice cubes to brighten winter days with this herbaceous and fizzy cocktail.* —Brooke

4 ounces gin
3 ounces fresh Meyer lemon juice
1½ ounces Meyer Lemon Simple Syrup (recipe on page 127)
Club soda, chilled
Garnish: Meyer lemon slice, fresh rosemary sprig

1. In a cocktail shaker, add gin, lemon juice, and Meyer Lemon Simple Syrup. Add ice and shake until cold. Strain into a chilled coupe glass. Top with club soda. Garnish with lemon and rosemary, if desired.

# BUTTERFLY

MAKES 1 SERVING

*This one's for you, Mom! If you have a copy of our last cocktail book,* Holiday Coupetails, *you've seen the Brandy Alexander that my mom loved so much . . . so why not take that same inspiration and create something even more "Mom-like" in her memory. Entrée Earl Grey tea, her absolute favorite. There is no doubt that butterflies will flutter around as this cocktail is made, Mom's sign to me that this would be her signature cocktail. And yes, Mom, this is more my kind of "teatime," and I'll always share it with you.* —Brian

1   bag Earl Grey tea*
2   ounces Cognac
1   ounce dark crème de cacao liqueur
1   ounce heavy whipping cream
Garnish: unsweetened cocoa powder

1. In a small bowl, combine tea bag and Cognac. Let steep for 30 minutes. Remove and discard tea bag, pressing bag to remove excess liquid.
2. In a cocktail shaker, add infused Cognac mixture, liqueur, and cream. Add ice and shake until cold. Strain into a coupe glass. Garnish with unsweetened cocoa powder, if desired.

*We used Brook37 The Atelier's Phyllis Earl Grey Bespoke Tea, a collaboration to honor Brian's mom, Phyllis Hoffman DePiano. It can be purchased on victoriamag.com/products.

# SWEET POTATO MARTINI

MAKES 1 SERVING

*Your eyes didn't deceive you, and it is not a typo. Thanks to the amazing Christa Cotton and her team at El Guapo, we have a sweet potato syrup that pairs perfectly with vodka to create this unique cocktail inspired by none other than my official food of the Thanksgiving table: Sweet Potato Casserole. Now, get some marshmallows ready, because how could you not want to toast them up for this one?* —Brian

2½ ounces vodka
½ ounce El Guapo Sweet Potato Syrup
**Garnish: toasted marshmallow**

1. In a cocktail shaker, add vodka, syrup, and ice. Shake until cold. Garnish with toasted marshmallow, if desired.

# AMARETTO GINGER SOUR

MAKES 1 SERVING

*Neither of us has sipped an Amaretto Sour in a few decades, but when we began dreaming up recipes for this book, we knew we wanted to add a sophisticated spin to an old standby. Enter ginger in two forms: crystallized and syrup. You can thank us upon first sip.* —B+B

- 2 ounces almond-flavored liquer
- 2 teaspoons finely chopped crystallized ginger
- 1 ounce fresh lemon juice
- ½ ounce El Guapo Ginger Syrup

Garnish: half orange slice, Amarena wild cherries in syrup

1. In a cocktail shaker, add liqueur, crystallized ginger, lemon juice, ginger syrup, and ice. Shake until cold. Strain into a coupe glass. Garnish with orange slice and cherries, if desired.

# VANILLA MILK PUNCH

MAKES 1 SERVING

*I always think about my sister-in-law, Katie, anytime I partake in bourbon milk punch—a signature drink that was served at the brunch festivities leading up to my brother, Eric, and her nuptials in Saint Francisville, Louisiana. Warm notes from rum and bourbon are taken to a whole new level with the blissful touch of vanilla bean in this milk punch—perfectly suited for serving as an after-dinner drink! —Brian*

- 1 ounce bourbon
- 1 ounce dark rum
- 1 ounce Simple Syrup (recipe on page 125)
- ½ teaspoon vanilla bean paste
- 4 ounces whole milk, very cold

Garnish: grated fresh nutmeg

1. In a cocktail shaker, add bourbon, dark rum, Simple Syrup, vanilla bean paste, and milk. Add ice and shake until cold. Strain into a coupe glass. Garnish with nutmeg, if desired.

# WHITE NEGRONI

MAKES 1 SERVING

*Smoother and silkier than the classic, Lillet Blanc's sweet honey, candied orange blossom, and white floral elegance pair with Cocchi Americano's bitter herbs for a bright, refreshing cocktail. —B+B*

2 ounces Lillet Blanc
1½ ounces gin
1 ounce Cocchi Americano
**Garnish: lemon twist**

1. In a cocktail shaker, add Lillet Blanc, gin, and Cocchi Americano. Add ice and shake until cold. Strain into a coupe glass. Garnish with lemon twist, if desired.

*Note: Cocchi Americano is a bitter, apéritif wine found in most large retailers.*

# JOANN'S AMERICANO

MAKES 1 SERVING

*This one is for our dear friend and fabulous Paris-based photographer, Joann Pai. She loves to toast the end of a photo shoot day with an Americano, the Negroni's younger, bubblier cousin.* —*B+B*

1½ ounces Campari
1½ ounces sweet vermouth
Club soda, chilled
Garnish: orange twist

1. In a mixing glass, add Campari, vermouth, and ice. Stir until cold. Strain into a coupe glass. Top with club soda. Garnish with orange twist, if desired.

# FRENCH-ISH MANHATTAN

MAKES 1 SERVING

*When my friend David Lebovitz published a French Manhattan recipe in his book,* **Drinking French,** *he made it with Cognac and included a cherry garnish for a nod to the original. In my French-ish version inspired by his, I use bourbon (because I'm a bourbon boy and love its sweetness) and kept the nod to France with the Cointreau and sweet vermouth.* —Brian

1½   ounces bourbon
1½   ounces sweet vermouth
½    ounce Cointreau or Grand Marnier
1    dash orange bitters
½    teaspoon vanilla bean paste
Garnish: Maraschino cherry, charred orange rind

1. In a mixing glass, add bourbon, vermouth, Cointreau or Grand Marnier, bitters, and vanilla bean paste. Add ice and stir until chilled. Strain into a coupe glass. Garnish with Maraschino cherry and orange rind, if desired.

# ROB ROY

MAKES 1 SERVING

*When we visited Perthshire in the Scottish Highlands last January for photo shoots, we spent a day at Ballintaggart with the family that dreamed up their incredible ecosystem that includes a picturesque farmhouse cooking school, general stores, hotel, and more. When we stopped by The Grandtully Hotel, we immediately admired co-owner Andrew Rowley's coupe collection on display in a cozy nook and started talking about our love for the glass and cocktails. We're honored that Andrew shared his Rob Roy cocktail with us, a perfect nod to beautiful Scotland. —B+B*

- 2 ounces good-quality single malt whiskey*
- ½ ounce Prune-Infused Sweet Vermouth (recipe follows)
- ½ ounce Pineapple Simple Syrup (recipe on page 127)
- 2 dashes pimiento bitters

Garnish: expressed orange zest

1. In a mixing glass, combine whiskey, Prune-Infused Sweet Vermouth, Pineapple Simple Syrup, and bitters. Add ice and stir until chilled. Strain into a chilled coupe glass. Garnish with orange zest, if desired.

*We used Finn Thomson Tomatin 2015.

**PRUNE-INFUSED SWEET VERMOUTH** Combine 2 cups quality sweet vermouth and ½ cup dried prunes in an airtight container. Let stand at room temperature for 48 hours. Strain, discarding prunes. Chill until ready to serve.

*Recipe courtesy of Andrew Rowley, Ballintaggart, Grandtully, Scotland*

# SWEET DAYS

BECAUSE YOU CAN'T
JUST DRINK OUT
OF YOUR COUPES

Chapter

4

# ESPRESSO MARTINI POTS DE CRÈME

MAKES 4 TO 6 SERVINGS

*Rich, silky chocolate spiked with espresso is topped with soft whipped cream and finished with espresso beans. Why not be extra? We are. —B+B*

- 5 large egg yolks (95 grams), room temperature
- 2 tablespoons (8 grams) instant espresso powder
- ¼ teaspoon kosher salt
- 1½ cups (360 grams) heavy whipping cream
- 12 ounces (340 grams) white chocolate, chopped
- 2 teaspoons (8 grams) vanilla extract
- ½ cup (120 grams) cold heavy whipping cream
- Garnish: chocolate-covered espresso beans

1. In a medium saucepan, whisk together yolks, espresso powder, and salt until combined. Add cream. Cook over medium-low heat until mixture thickens, coats the back of a spoon, and reaches 175°F to 180°F, 8 to 10 minutes.
2. Remove from heat and strain through a fine-mesh sieve. Whisk in chopped chocolate and vanilla until smooth. Divide evenly between coupe glasses. Refrigerate until set, at least 4 hours or up to overnight.
3. When ready to serve, in a large bowl using a balloon whisk, whisk cold heavy whipping cream until cream is just slightly thickened and pourable, about 1 minute. Spoon soft cream over pots de crème. Garnish with espresso beans, if desired.

# LEMON POSSET

MAKES ABOUT 6 SERVINGS

*Bright, velvety smooth, and unapologetically luscious—our Lemon Posset is served in a coupe glass (obviously!) instead of the traditional lemon rind. We promise it will make your taste buds do a happy dance. —B+B*

- 2 cups (480 grams) heavy whipping cream
- ¾ cup (150 grams) granulated sugar
- 2 tablespoons (5 grams) lightly packed lemon zest
- ⅓ cup (80 grams) fresh lemon juice

Garnish: lemon peel twists, Meringue Kisses (recipe on page 121)

1. In a small saucepan, bring cream and sugar to a gentle boil over medium heat, stirring often. Remove from heat and stir in lemon zest and juice. Let cool for about 10 minutes, stirring occasionally. Divide evenly into coupe glasses. Refrigerate for at least 4 hours, or up to overnight.
2. When ready to serve, garnish with a lemon twist and a Meringue Kiss. Keep refrigerated for up to 3 days.

# NO-BAKE CHEESECAKE

MAKES 4 TO 6 SERVINGS

*Decadent no-bake cheesecake topped with a bold, tart cherry filling—a perfect mix of indulgence and nostalgia in every spoonful. —B+B*

**Crust**
- ½ cup (60 grams) graham cracker crumbs
- 2 tablespoons (28 grams) unsalted butter, melted
- ¼ teaspoon kosher salt

**Filling**
- 4 ounces (113 grams) cream cheese, softened
- ½ cup (100 grams) granulated sugar
- 1½ teaspoons (9 grams) vanilla bean paste
- 1 cup (240 grams) cold heavy whipping cream

Bonne Maman Cherry Pie Filling, to top

1. For the crust: In a medium bowl, stir together graham cracker crumbs, melted butter, and salt until combined. Divide between coupe glasses, about 2 tablespoons (15 grams) each.

2. For the filling: In the bowl of a stand mixer fitted with the whisk attachment, beat cream cheese, sugar, and vanilla bean paste on medium speed until sugar is dissolved. With the mixer on low speed, slowly add cold heavy whipping cream. Stop the mixer and thoroughly scrape down bottom and sides of the bowl. Slowly increase mixer speed to medium high and beat until stiff peaks form.

3. Spoon filling into a piping bag fitted with a large open round tip*. Pipe filling into each glass and spread with an offset spatula as desired. Refrigerate until ready to serve, at least 1 hour.

4. When ready to serve, top each cheesecake with Bonne Maman Cherry Pie Filling. Refrigerate, covered, for up to 3 days.

*We used Ateco #808.

# POUND CAKE WITH BERRIES & ANGLAISE

MAKES 6 TO 8 SERVINGS

*As Southerners, pound cake is a humble staple we'll never quit. We love elevating it with fresh berries and pouring crème anglaise tableside for that extra wow factor.* —B+B

- ¾ cup (170 grams) unsalted butter, softened
- 1¼ cups (250 grams) granulated sugar
- 3 large eggs (150 grams), room temperature
- 2 teaspoons (8 grams) vanilla extract
- 1⅔ cups (208 grams) all-purpose flour
- ½ teaspoon (1.5 grams) kosher salt
- ¼ teaspoon (1.25 grams) baking powder
- ½ cup (120 grams) whole milk, room temperature
- 1½ cups (300 grams) mixed berries
- Crème Anglaise (recipe on page 120)

**1.** Preheat oven to 350°F (180°C). Spray a 9x5-inch loaf pan with baking spray with flour and line with parchment paper so that it extends over the two long sides.

**2.** In the bowl of a stand mixer fitted with the paddle attachment, beat butter and sugar at medium speed until fluffy, 5 to 7 minutes, stopping to scrape sides of bowl. Reduce mixer speed to low. Add eggs, one at a time, beating well after each addition. Beat in vanilla.

**3.** In a medium bowl, whisk together flour, salt, and baking powder. Gradually add flour mixture to butter mixture alternating with milk, beginning and ending with flour mixture, beating just until combined after each addition. Pour batter into prepared pan. Firmly tap pan on counter to settle batter.

**4.** Bake until a wooden pick inserted near center comes out clean, 50 minutes to 1 hour. Let cool in pan for 10 minutes. Remove from pan, and let cool completely on a wire rack.

**5.** When ready to serve, cut the cake into 1½-inch cubes. Layer cakes cubes evenly on the bottom of coupe glasses. Just when ready to serve, top with berries and Crème Anglaise.

# ETON MESS

MAKES ABOUT 6 SERVINGS

*This is one dessert we always order, if we see it on the menu, and a mess we'll always be in favor of. Crisp and crunchy Meringue Kisses are layered with fluffy whipped cream and bright strawberries for a dessert that's full of texture and flavor. —B+B*

| | |
|---|---|
| 1 | pound (454 grams) fresh strawberries, hulled and diced |
| 2 | tablespoons (25 grams) granulated sugar |
| 2 | teaspoons (2 grams) lemon zest |
| 1½ | cups (360 grams) cold heavy whipping cream |

Meringue Kisses (recipe on page 121)

1. In a medium bowl, stir together strawberries, sugar, and lemon zest. Let stand to macerate for at least 30 minutes, stirring occasionally.
2. In the bowl of a stand mixer fitted with a whisk attachment, beat cold heavy cream until medium peaks form, 2 to 4 minutes.
3. In each coupe glass, dollop 3 tablespoons (20 grams) whipped cream. Top with 2 tablespoons (32 grams) macerated strawberry mixture and 3 to 4 Meringue Kisses. Repeat layer once more. Top with more Meringue Kisses and crumble one over the top of each to garnish, if desired. Serve immediately.

# RUM RAISIN RICE PUDDING

MAKES ABOUT 5 CUPS

*Rice pudding is comfort food... in dessert form. Rum and raisins are a classic combination, and when paired with warm spices, this modest dessert gives you a big hug like you're sitting fireside with a cozy blanket.* —B+B

- 1 cup (93 grams) golden raisins
- ½ cup (120 grams) black rum
- 1 tablespoon (12 grams) firmly packed light brown sugar
- 4 cups (960 grams) whole milk
- 1 cup (240 grams) heavy whipping cream
- ¾ cup (165 grams) Arborio rice (or other medium-grain rice)
- ¾ cup (150 grams) granulated sugar
- 1 teaspoon (4 grams) vanilla extract
- ½ teaspoon (1.5 grams) kosher salt
- ¼ teaspoon ground nutmeg
- ¼ teaspoon ground cinnamon

1. In a small saucepan, combine raisins, rum, and brown sugar. Bring to a gentle boil over medium heat, stirring occasionally. Remove from heat and cover. Let stand until the raisins have plumped up significantly and absorbed most of the rum, at least 1 hour or preferably overnight for the most plump raisins.

2. In a large saucepan, combine whole milk, cream, rice, granulated sugar, vanilla, and salt. Bring to a gentle boil over medium-high heat. Reduce to a simmer over medium-low heat and cook, stirring often, until the rice is tender and mixture is thick, about 20 to 25 minutes. (Mixture will be very saucy but will continue to absorb liquid.) Remove from heat.

3. Stir in soaked raisins with nutmeg, cinnamon, and any remaining rum. Serve warm or cover and refrigerate until ready to serve. Refrigerate in an airtight container for up to 3 days.

# BANANA PUDDING

MAKES ABOUT 4 SERVINGS

*Potluck, but make it elegant! Keeping it classic with cooked custard, bananas, and Nilla Wafers transports me back to my mom's kitchen with each bite—and no need to get your Pyrex casserole dish out for this one. Coupe glasses and toasted Swiss Meringue take this comfort food dessert to new heights. I mean, look at the avant-garde swath of meringue serving fabulousness on those!* —Brian

- ¼ cup (50 grams) granulated sugar
- 1½ tablespoons (12 grams) cornstarch
- ¼ teaspoon kosher salt
- 3 large egg yolks (56 grams)
- 1½ cups (360 grams) whole milk
- 2 tablespoons (28 grams) unsalted butter, softened
- ½ teaspoon (3 grams) vanilla bean paste
- Mini vanilla wafer cookies, whole and lightly crushed
- 2 to 3 very ripe medium bananas
- Swiss Meringue (recipe on page 121)

**1.** In a medium bowl, whisk together sugar, cornstarch, and salt. Whisk in egg yolks until well combined. (Mixture will be very thick.)

**2.** In a medium saucepan, heat milk over medium heat until steaming. (Do not boil.) Gradually add half of warm milk to sugar mixture, whisking constantly. Add sugar mixture to remaining warm milk in pan. Bring to a boil over medium heat, whisking constantly, until thickened and until mixture is no longer starchy, about 3 to 4 minutes. Remove from heat.

**3.** Add butter to warm milk mixture in two additions, stirring until combined; stir in vanilla bean paste. Pour and press mixture through fine-mesh sieve into a heatproof bowl. Let cool completely, stirring occasionally to prevent a skin from forming, about 30 minutes.

*(continued on page 120)*

# CHOCOLATE MOUSSE

MAKES ABOUT 6 SERVINGS

*I've recently been on a mission to recreate a chocolate mousse based on one served at a favorite restaurant in Paris (no, I can't reveal the name so I can continue to get a reservation!). It's served family style in a large bowl with a ladle so you can help yourself as many times as you'd like until the bowl is empty. My ideal French-style mousse is sticky, full of air bubbles, and just chocolate. No coffee. No Grand Marnier. When I presented this to my family last Christmas in an antique French ironstone terrine, they declared it the best holiday dessert ever.* —Brooke

- 5 ounces (142 grams) chopped bittersweet chocolate
- 3 ounces (85 grams) chopped milk chocolate
- 1½ tablespoons (21 grams) unsalted butter
- 4 large eggs (200 grams), separated
- ½ cup (100 grams) granulated sugar, divided
- ¾ cup (180 grams) heavy whipping cream
- 1½ teaspoons (6 grams) vanilla extract
- Garnish: unsweetened cocoa powder, chocolate curls

1. In a large heatproof bowl over a simmering water bath, melt chocolates and butter. Remove from heat. Let stand until cool to the touch.
2. While chocolate is cooling, separate eggs into two medium bowls. Using a hand mixer, beat whites on medium speed until they start to foam, about 1 minute. Slowly add ¼ cup (50 grams) sugar, then increase speed to high and beat until stiff peaks form, 7 to 8 minutes.

*(continued on page 120)*

## BANANA PUDDING
*(continued from page 116)*

**4.** To assemble, spread 2 tablespoons (32 grams) pudding into the bottom of each coupe glass. Cover with 1 layer of vanilla wafer cookies and a layer of banana slices. Repeat layering, ending with a top layer of pudding. Refrigerate until thoroughly chilled, 2 to 3 hours, or up to overnight. (Assembled Banana Pudding without Swiss Meringue can be refrigerated in an airtight container for up to 3 days.)
**5.** When ready to serve, top with Swiss Meringue, using a handheld torch to gently brown meringue, if desired.

## CHOCOLATE MOUSSE
*(continued from page 119)*

**3.** Beat yolks on medium speed until they start to thicken, about 1 minute. Slowly add remaining ¼ cup (50 grams) sugar, then increase speed to medium-high and beat until thick and ribbon-like, 2 to 3 minutes.
**4.** In a separate bowl, beat heavy cream and vanilla on high until stiff peaks form, about 2 to 3 minutes.
**5.** Once chocolate is cool, gently fold in yolks until completely combined. Then gently fold in whites, then whipped cream. Divide mixture evenly between coupe glasses. Refrigerate until set, at least 4 hours or up to overnight.
**6.** When ready to serve, dust lightly with cocoa powder and garnish with chocolate curls.

## CRÈME ANGLAISE
MAKES ABOUT 2 CUPS

| | |
|---|---|
| ⅔ | cup (160 grams) heavy whipping cream |
| ⅔ | cup (160 grams) whole milk |
| ½ | cup (100 grams) granulated sugar, divided |
| 2 | teaspoons (12 grams) vanilla bean paste |
| ½ | teaspoon (1.5 grams) kosher salt |
| 4 | large egg yolks (72 grams), room temperature |

**1.** In a medium saucepan, heat cream, milk, ¼ cup (50 grams) sugar, vanilla bean paste, and salt over medium-low heat, stirring frequently, just until steaming (do not boil).
**2.** Meanwhile, in a medium bowl, whisk together egg yolks and remaining ¼ cup (50 grams) sugar.
**3.** Slowly pour approximately half of warm cream mixture into egg mixture, whisking constantly. Add egg mixture to remaining warm cream mixture, whisking to combine. Cook, whisking constantly, until mixture starts to thicken and coats the back of a spoon and an instant-read thermometer registers 180°F (82°C).
**4.** Immediately strain into a fine-mesh sieve over a medium bowl. Place bowl in an ice bath to cool quickly, or cover with a piece of plastic wrap, placing wrap directly onto surface, and refrigerate. Store in the refrigerator for up to 4 days.

## SWISS MERINGUE
MAKES ABOUT 3 CUPS

- ¾ cup (150 grams) granulated sugar
- 3 large egg whites (90 grams), room temperature
- ¼ teaspoon kosher salt
- ¼ teaspoon cream of tartar
- 1 teaspoon (4 grams) vanilla extract

**1.** In the heatproof bowl of a stand mixer, whisk together sugar, egg whites, salt, and cream of tartar. Cook, stirring occasionally, over simmering water until an instant-read thermometer registers 160°F (70°C).

**2.** Carefully move bowl to stand mixer fitted with the whisk attachment. Beat on high speed until mixture has cooled and tripled in volume, 5 to 7 minutes. Beat in vanilla extract. Use immediately.

## MERINGUE KISSES
MAKES ABOUT 50 KISSES

- 3 large egg whites (90 grams), room temperature
- ¼ teaspoon cream of tartar
- ¼ teaspoon kosher salt
- ¾ cup (150 grams) granulated sugar
- ¼ teaspoon (1 gram) vanilla extract

**1.** In the bowl of a stand mixer fitted with the whisk attachment, beat egg whites, cream of tartar, and salt at medium-low speed until soft peaks form, 4 to 5 minutes. With mixer on low speed, add sugar in a slow, steady stream, beating until combined. (This should take about 2 minutes.) Increase mixer speed to medium, and beat until thick and shiny, 7 to 8 minutes, stopping to scrape sides of bowl halfway through mixing. Rub meringue between 2 fingers to make sure it is smooth and no sugar granules remain. Add vanilla, and beat at medium-high speed until combined, about 30 seconds.

**2.** Preheat oven to 225°F (107°C). Line 2 baking sheets with parchment paper.

**3.** Transfer meringue to a large pastry bag fitted with a ½-inch opening French Star piping tip*. Holding tip perpendicular to parchment paper, pipe small meringue kisses at least ½ inch apart on prepared pans.

**4.** Bake until dry to the touch, 45 minutes to 1 hour. Turn oven off, and let meringue kisses cool completely in oven overnight with door closed. Alternately, let cool in oven with the door closed for at least 1 hour; remove from oven (meringues will peel off parchment without sticking), and let cool completely on pans.

*We used Ateco #866.

# SIMPLE SYRUPS

Don't waste your money on the store-bought stuff when Simple Syrup is easy (and cheap!) to make at home. We love how customizable the recipe is, and the syrup lasts in your fridge for weeks to use over and over again.

In a medium saucepan, combine 2 cups water and 1 cup granulated sugar; cook over medium heat, stirring frequently, until sugar dissolves. Remove from heat and let cool completely at room temperature. Refrigerate in an airtight container up to 2 weeks.

## BLUEBERRY-VANILLA SIMPLE SYRUP
MAKES ABOUT 1 CUP

- 1    cups granulated sugar
- 1    cup water
- 1    cup fresh blueberries
- 1    tablespoon vanilla paste

**1.** In a medium saucepan over medium heat, bring sugar, water, and blueberries to a boil, stirring frequently; boil until sugar dissolves, about 1 minute. Remove from heat and let cool completely at room temperature. Stir in vanilla bean paste. Using a fine-mesh strainer, strain into an airtight container. Refrigerate until ready to serve, up to 1 month.

## DEMERARA SIMPLE SYRUP
MAKES ABOUT 1 CUP

- 1    cup demerara sugar
- 1    cup water

**1.** In a medium saucepan over medium heat, bring all ingredients to a boil, stirring frequently; boil until sugar dissolves, about 1 minute. Remove from heat and let cool completely at room temperature. Refrigerate in an airtight container until ready to serve, up to 2 weeks.

## PEACH SIMPLE SYRUP
MAKES ABOUT 1 CUP

- 2    cups water
- 1    cup granulated sugar
- 2    large peaches chopped (leave the skin on)

**1.** In a medium saucepan over medium heat, cook water, sugar, and peaches until peaches fall apart, about 10 minutes. Remove from heat and cool completely at room temperature. Using a fine-mesh strainer, strain into an airtight container. Refrigerate until ready to serve, up to 2 weeks.

## SPICED SIMPLE SYRUP
MAKES ABOUT 1 CUP

- 1    cup granulated sugar
- 1    cup water
- 6    whole cloves
- 2    star anise
- 2    cinnamon sticks
- 2    juniper berries

**1.** In a medium saucepan over medium heat, bring sugar and water to a boil, stirring frequently; boil until sugar dissolves, about 1 minute. Remove from heat and add cloves, star anise, cinnamon, and juniper. Let cool completely at room temperature. Refrigerate in an airtight container, up to 2 weeks.

## PEAR THYME SIMPLE SYRUP
MAKES ABOUT 1 CUP

- 1 cup granulated sugar
- 1 cup water
- 1 medium Bartlett pear, cored and chopped

1. In a medium saucepan over medium heat, bring all ingredients to a boil, stirring frequently; boil until sugar dissolves, about 1 minute. Remove from heat and let cool completely at room temperature. Refrigerate in an airtight container until ready to serve, up to 1 month.

## THYME SIMPLE SYRUP
MAKES ABOUT 1 CUP

1 cup granulated sugar
1 cup water
1 bunch fresh thyme

1. In a medium saucepan over medium heat, bring sugar and water to a boil, stirring frequently; boil until sugar dissolves, about 1 minute. Remove from heat and add thyme. Let cool completely at room temperature. Refrigerate in an airtight container until ready to serve, up to 2 weeks.

## MEYER LEMON SIMPLE SYRUP
MAKES ABOUT 1 CUP

- 1 cup granulated sugar
- 1 cup water
- 2 fresh springs rosemary
- 2 fresh strips Meyer lemon zest

1. In a medium saucepan over medium heat, bring all ingredients to a boil, stirring frequently; boil until sugar dissolves, about 1 minute. Remove from heat and let cool completely at room temperature. Using a fine-mesh strainer, strain into an airtight container. Refrigerate until ready to serve, up to 2 weeks.

## PINEAPPLE SIMPLE SYRUP*
MAKES ABOUT 1½ CUPS

1½ cups sugar
1¼ cups pressed fresh pineapple juice

1. In a medium saucepan over medium heat, bring all ingredients to a boil, stirring frequently; boil until sugar dissolves, about 1 minute. Remove from heat and let cool completely at room temperature. Refrigerate in an airtight container until ready to serve, up to 2 weeks.

*Recipe courtesy of Andrew Rowley, Ballintaggart, Grandtully, Scotland

# FLAVOR-PACKED ICE CUBES

For larger fruit like strawberries and limes, cut into smaller slices. Place into ice cube mold. Top with distilled water. Freeze until firm.

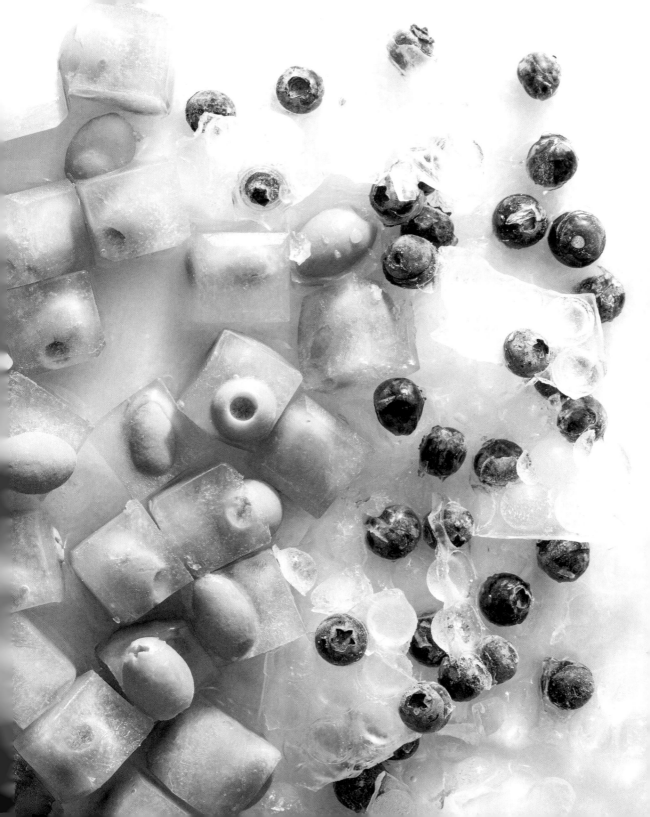

# ACKNOWLEDGMENTS

Everything I do in this life is a tribute to **my incredible mom, Phyllis Norton Hoffman DePiano**. She was hands down the most talented person I've ever known, and she passed down to me the joy of creating beauty and carving out new paths. Oh, and let's not forget—she gifted me a lot of the coupes you'll find throughout this book. So, whenever I raise a glass, it's for her. The Butterfly cocktail? All hers. Here's to the absolute hero of my life.

**To my husband, Stephen:** Thanks for letting me "borrow" your famous cocktails one more time. I treasure our cocktail hours and the calm they bring into our lives. Your constant love and support are everything.

**To my twin brother, Eric:** Sure, we share a birthday, but that's where the similarities end. When I reach for vodka, he's over there with his gin. He sips rosé in the evenings and cold days, while I'm basking in the sunshine of spring and summer with my rosé. He's the CEO, all business with his "budget" and "projections," while I'm out here chasing inspiration and going with my gut. But honestly, without him, there wouldn't be a business. Thank you for believing in my vision, for being the best brother, and for helping keep mom's legacy alive. It's an honor to do it by your side.

**To Paris:** The City of Light, the heartbeat of my soul, my heart home. And those antique markets? Don't even get me started. They're overflowing with the coupes I can't resist collecting. Every time I go, I understand why Gertrude Stein said, "America is my country and Paris is my hometown." When I'm there, my creativity soars, and I find a side of myself I never knew existed.

**Lastly, to Brooke:** My work wife, my partner-in-crime, and the most imaginative soul I know . . . How fun is it to scribble ideas on hotel notepads and then watch them turn into something real? I still can't believe you only had your first martini two years ago, but I'm so glad you did. That martini at the Hemingway Bar in Paris? It sparked the brainstorm that brought this book to life. So, merci mon ami—what a ride it's been.

— *Brian*

**To my dad,** who's been in my thoughts a lot during the creation of this book, for instilling in me the appreciation of a good Bushwacker. I wish we could drink another one together.

**To my husband, Andy,** for always seeking out the best cocktail spots when we travel, and for making cocktail hours at home cherished time together.

**To my other husband (my work husband, that is!), Brian,** for being my creative counterpart for the last 18 years and for loving a good hotel bar sit as much as I do. It's a good thing we're just getting started!

— *Brooke*

---

**To Vanessa Rocchio:** Our fellow cocktail enthusiast, you took our wild flavor dreams and travel-inspired cravings and turned them into cocktails that are destined to be classics.

**For our photographer, Stephanie Steele:** Affectionately known as "Freckles," you bring sunshine to cloudy days. Your lens doesn't miss — and neither does your fierce dedication.

**To all of our colleagues who helped bring this book to life:** Seriously, how lucky are we? We get to call this a job, drinking cocktails as research. You can't make this up.

— *B + B*

# INDEX

### BOURBON & WHISKY
French-ish Manhattan 99
Peach Old Fashioned 65
Rob Roy 100
Vanilla Milk Punch 92

### CHAMPAGNE
Sabrina 31
Strawberry Sparkler 62

### COGNAC
Butterfly 87
French Negroni 27

### GIN
In a Pickle 70
Peach Gin Smash 41
Pear Thyme Gimlet 80
Rabbit Rabbit 23
Rosemary Meyer Lemon Gin Fizz 84
Spanish Gin and Tonic 45
Stephen's Ginger Martini 76
The English Tea 28
Tom Collins 24
Tomato Martini 42

### LIMONCELLO & LIQUEURS
Amaretto Ginger Sour 91
Joann's Americano 96
Limoncello Spritz 61

### RUM
Bushwacker 50
Clarified Piña Colada 54
Not Frozen Piña Colada 54
Rum Reverie 66

### SWEETS
Banana Pudding 116

Chocolate Mousse 119
Crème Anglaise 120
Espresso Martini Pots de Crème 104
Lemon Posset 107
Meringue Kisses 121
No-Bake Cheesecake 109
Poundcake with Berries & Anglaise 110
Rum Raisin Rice Pudding 115
Swiss Meringue 121

### TEQUILA AND MEZCAL
Not So Sweet Tequila Sunrise 58
Orange Hibiscus Margarita 73
Sunset Sizzle 69

### VODKA
Blackberry Bramble 46
Blueberry Lemon Drop 38
Concord Crush 83
Dirty Martini 19
End of the Jam Jar Martini 35
Jardin Secret 53
La Vie en Rosé 57
Nitro Cold Brew Martini 32
The Orange Thing 20
Sweet Potato Martini 88
The Wing View 16

### WINE
Peach Daydream 49
Spiced Lillet Rouge 79
White Negroni 95

### ALL THE REST
Blackberry Vodka 54
Blueberry-Vanilla Simple Syrup 126
Cherry Reduction 73
Concord Grape Purée 90
Demerara Simple Syrup 126

Fruit Ice Cubes 128
Hibiscus Sugar 110
Homemade Grenadine 42
Meyer Lemon Simple Syrup 127
Peach Simple Syrup 126
Pear Thyme Simple Syrup 127
Pineapple Simple Syrup 127
Prune-Infused Sweet Vermouth 38
Simple Syrup 125
Spiced Simple Syrup 126
Strawberry Purée 66
Thyme Simple Syrup 127
Tomato Liquid 42

### CREDITS:

**83 PRESS EDITORIAL**
Editorial Director: Marie Baxley
Senior Editor: Kristi Fleetwood
Copy Editor: Adrienne Davis
Art Director: Karissa Brown
Senior Digital Imaging Specialist:
  Delisa McDaniel
Test Kitchen Director: Laura Crandall
Recipe Testers/Developers/Stylists:
Katie Moon Dickerson, Vanessa
  Rocchio, Amanda Stabile
Photographer: Stephanie Welbourne-Steele
Contributing Photographer:
  Kyle Carpenter
Prop Stylist: Mary Beth Jones
Contributing Prop Stylist:
  Maggie Hill Ratliff and
  Vanessa Rocchio

### VERY SPECIAL THANKS

To our friends at El Guapo (elguapobitters.com) for stocking our bar with amazing bitters and syrups.

Williams Sonoma (williams-sonoma.com) for making sure we're always outfitted with the best barware.

Bobbins Design (bobbinsdesign.com) for making our cocktail hours stylish with the best linens.